D0177139

IT'S NEVER TOO EARLY
TO FIND OUT ABOUT...

THE
GARDEN

IT'S NEVER TOO EARLY
TO FIND OUT ABOUT . . .
THE
GARDEN

Written by
LOUISA LEAMAN

Illustrated by
NATASHA RIMMINGTON

Orion
Children's Books

First published in Great Britain in 2015 by Orion Children's Books
An imprint of Hachette Children's Group
and published by Hodder and Stoughton Ltd
338 Euston Road
London NW1 3BH
An Hachette UK Company

1 3 5 7 9 10 8 6 4 2

Text © Louisa Leaman 2015
Illustrations © Natasha Rimmington 2015

The right of Louisa Leaman and Natasha Rimmington to be
identified as author and illustrator of this work has been asserted.

ISBN 978 1 4440 1546 1

For Tove and Harper

CONTENTS

1
What's in a Garden?

Do you have a garden?
You might have a little one or a big one.
You might share a garden with your
neighbours. Or maybe your garden is
a flower box on a balcony.

Gardens provide homes
for lots of different wildlife,

like birds,

insects,

squirrels

or fish.

The flowers in your garden are a home for insects. Ladybirds, butterflies, ants, beetles, flies and spiders are all common garden insects.

You will spot different flowers in your garden
at different times of the year.

spring

summer

autumn

winter

14

Some birds you might see in your garden
are woodpigeons, robins, blackbirds,
magpies and blue tits.

If you're lucky, you might have a bird's nest. Robins like to build nests in strange places – sheds, hanging baskets, even the pocket of some trousers left on a washing line!

Do you have a garden pond?
A pond is a home for fish.
It's also a home for lots of different
plants and insects, like pond skaters
and dragonflies.

You might also see frogs and newts.
They are **amphibians** (am-fib-ee-uns) and
can live on land and in water.

The green stuff floating on your pond is **algae** (al-gee). Some scientists think algae are one of the most important life forms on Earth because they create oxygen, which humans need to breathe. So, if you have a pond with algae, you are helping yourself to survive!

2
A Garden in Spring

Spring is a time for new life and new beginnings. Birds sing, flowers grow and buds appear on trees.

The garden wakes up after winter.
Days are longer and warmer because
the Earth has turned and is tilting towards
the sun. And did you know, when it's spring
and summer where you live, it's winter on
the other side of the world!

Birdsong is one of the first signs of spring.
Many birds, like swallows and warblers,
fly to warmer places during the winter
months, and come back in spring to find
a mate and have babies.

You might be lucky enough to find
an eggshell, which means a baby bird
has hatched!

It isn't just birds that have babies
in the spring. If you have a pond,
you might see spawn and tadpoles. These
are baby frogs and newts.

Spring is a good time to sow seeds in the ground, because the warm weather makes them **germinate** (jer-min-ate) and start growing upwards towards the sun. If you look closely, you might see little green seedlings bursting out of the earth.

Early spring flowers are
crocuses and daffodils.

Some trees, like apple trees and cherry trees, grow blossom. Blossom on the trees is another sign that spring is here.

Blossom and flowers attract insects like bees and butterflies with their bright colours and smells. Insects help with **pollination** (poll-in-ay-shun), which is how plants make seeds and survive.

Bees are good pollinators.
When a bee visits a flower
looking for sweet nectar to eat,
pollen gets caught on its body.
When the bee visits another
flower, the pollen rubs off and
touches the **stigma**, which
is the flower's egg. When the
pollen and the egg meet,
a new seed starts
to grow.

27

Birds, bats and the wind
can also take pollen between plants.

28

Oak trees, pine trees and maple trees have acorns, pinecones and catkins, which get blown from the branches and settle in the ground and grow.

Do you know anyone with hay fever?
They probably suffer most in spring,
because this is when lots of pollen
is blowing through the air!

3
A Garden in Summer

Summer is a time for sunshine and colour.
In summer, people say the garden is in
full bloom. The days are longer and
the sky is blue.

Look out of the window. The long hours of daylight have made everything grow. The buds on the trees have turned into leaves. The little seedlings have grown into flowers.

Plants need sunlight in order to grow and stay alive. **Chlorophyll** (klo-ro-fill) is a chemical in plants' leaves that turns sunlight into food and keeps them green.

Summer flowers have colourful petals, like honeysuckle, roses, jasmine and sweetpeas. The bright colours and smells attract insects. If you look closely at a flowerbed in summer, you will see lots of different insects.

As the weather gets warmer you might see more butterflies. Butterflies prefer summer weather because the heat helps their wings to move. If it is too cold, they can't fly.

In the summer heat, flowers and trees get thirsty, just like humans. They have roots under the ground, which suck up water from the soil, like a drinking straw.

Sunlight makes weeds grow too. Weeds steal nutrients from flowers and trees, so gardeners like to get rid of them. A common summer weed is the stinging nettle. Its leaves are covered in tiny hairs. The hairs contain chemicals that cause a painful sting when touched.

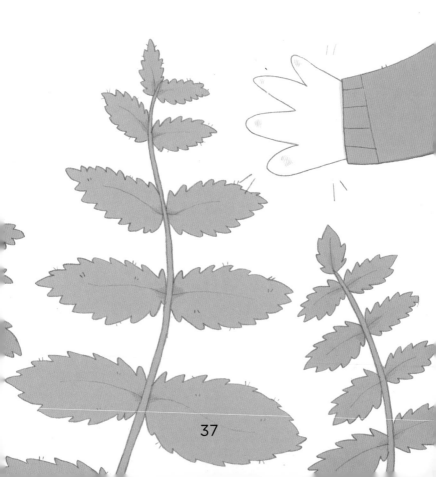

But did you know, stinging nettle leaves
are also used to make nettle tea?

4
A Garden in Autumn

Autumn is a time of change, as plants and animals get ready for winter.

In autumn, the earth tilts away from the sun
and the weather gets cooler again.
The leaves on the trees are turning
golden brown.

This is because the shorter days tell the trees that it is time to stop feeding and growing for the winter. The **chlorophyll**, the special chemical in their leaves, fades away because it isn't needed.

When the leaves turn brown, they dry up and fall to the ground. Fallen leaves are a home for insects, such as spiders, beetles and caterpillars.

Remember the fruit trees in spring,
with their blossom? Thanks to **pollination**,
the blossom flowers have produced fruits,
like apples, pears and plums.

Some trees keep their leaves in autumn,
and stay green throughout the year.
These trees are called **evergreens**.

In the cool autumn weather animals and insects start storing food.

Honey bees go
into their hives
and make honey.

Squirrels bury nuts
underground.

Some birds begin their long journey to warmer countries, where food will be plentiful. This is called **migrating** (my-gray-ting).

Insects aren't as busy in the autumn, because there are fewer flowers. Many flowers die because they can't survive the colder weather. They leave behind seeds, which will grow into new flowers in the spring.

In the autumn, you might see gardeners digging the ground, before it gets hard with frost. Many gardeners add compost as they dig. Compost is food for plants. It provides extra nutrients to help growth.

Did you know compost can be made from your dinner? You can recycle your leftover food, along with grass cuttings, cardboard, and fallen leaves.

In autumn, you will see lots of worms.
Worms live underground, where it's damp
and dark. They burrow through soil, then eat
and poo it out! This may sound a bit yucky,
but it helps keep the soil crumbly,
and is good for growing plants.

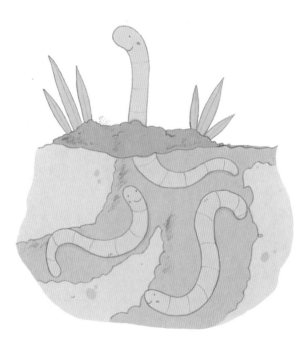

5
A Garden in Winter

Winter is a time of rest. The days are short and temperatures are very low. The garden may seem quiet, but there is a lot going on.

Look out of your window.
The tree branches are bare, but they
aren't dead. They are resting and will
grow again in the spring.

Maybe you have a pine tree in your garden? This is a type of **evergreen** and keeps its leaves all year round. Pine trees are popular at Christmas, when people like to decorate them.

When the weather gets very cold,
your pond might freeze over. Underneath,
the frogs, fish and newts will be hiding at
the bottom, where the water is warmest.
They stay very still to save energy.

In the winter, it might snow.
Did you know that no two snowflakes
are alike?

When snow covers the ground, it is the hardest time for animals to find food. Some don't eat at all. Instead, they go to sleep for the winter. We call this **hibernation** (hy-ber-nay-shun).

Did you know that a snail hibernates in its own shell? It curls up and doesn't move or eat for months.

Many birds, like swallows and swifts, migrate.
Some birds, like blackbirds and robins,
stay if they can find enough to eat.
Why not put a bird feeder out to
help them?

A garden in winter is a garden that is waiting. Soon another spring will come, and another year of growing and **pollinating** and blooming and feeding will begin again.

6
Some Words
You Might Not Know . . .

Algae – A green plant that grows
in your pond.

Bud – A new growth at the end of a branch
or stem that turns into a flower or leaf.

Blossom – Flowers that appear on plants
and trees and produce fruit.

Germination – The process by which a seed
grows into a plant.

Hibernation – A long, deep sleep, which allows animals to survive the winter.

Nectar – A sweet liquid produced by plants.

Nutrients – Chemicals in the environment that animals and plants need to help them grow.

Pollination – How pollen is transferred from one flower to another, enabling the plant to make seeds and survive.

Seed – A very young plant that is resting and covered in a protective coat.

Seedling – A young plant, raised from a seed.

WHAT WILL YOU

Dive into the deep dark sea.

Come face to face with incredible dinosaurs.

DISCOVER NEXT?

Take a look at your own back garden.

Speed off to outer space.

It's never too early to find out more.